Australia's Neighbours

Bangladesh

DISCOVER THE COUNTRY, CULTURE AND PEOPLE

Jane Hinchey

REDBACK publishing

First published 2019 by
Redback Publishing
PO Box 357 Frenchs Forest NSW 2086
Australia

www.redbackpublishing.com.au
orders@redbackpublishing.com.au

Reprinted 2023

ISBN 978-1-925860-66-5 PBK

Author: Jane Hinchey
Editor: Marianne Lindsell
Designer: Redback Publishing

Original illustrations © Redback Publishing 2023
Originated by Redback Publishing

Printed and bound in Malaysia

Acknowledgements
Abbreviations: l—left, r—right, b—bottom, t—top, c—centre, m—middle
We would like to thank the following for permission to reproduce photographs: (Images © shutterstock) p8 Dmitry Chulov, p9b Sk Hasan Ali, p10b StevenK, p11b Andrew V Marcus, p15b Pinar Alver, p17b Sk Hasan Ali, p18b Dmitry Chulov, 19t Sk Hasan Ali, p20b Passion Images, p23b Sk Hasan Ali, p24b zaferkizilkaya, p25t Denys Yelmanov, p28b Dietmar Temps, p29tr MASWENGS STUDIOS, p29b Dmitry Chulov

NATIONAL LIBRARY OF AUSTRALIA
A catalogue record for this book is available from the National Library of Australia

Contents

Map of Bangladesh

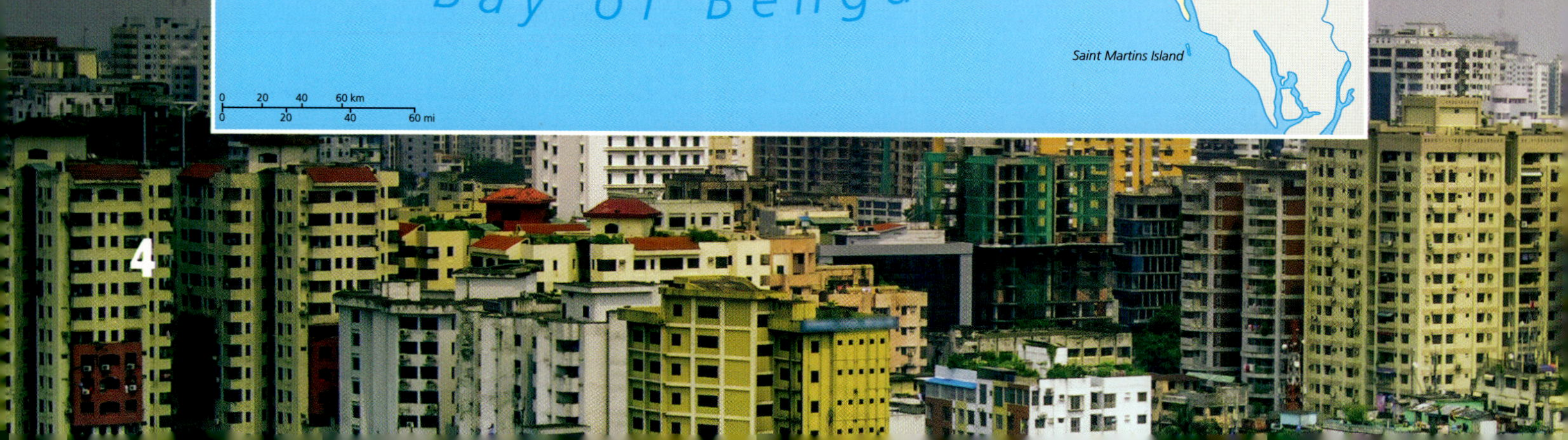

Snapshot

Official name:	People's Republic of Bangladesh
Population:	168,390,210 (2022)
Capital:	Dhaka
Land area:	147,570 square kilometres
Official language:	Bengali
Official Religion:	Islam
System of Government:	Unitary parliamentary republic
Currency:	Taka

MAJOR SITES

- Dhaka City
- Tangail
- Comilla
- Nawabganj
- Sonargaon
- Lalbagh Fort
- Mahasthangarh
- Tajhat Palace
- Cox's Bazar

Fun Facts

- The word Bangladesh means "the people of Bengal" in the local language.
- Cox's Bazar is a town with the longest beach in the world, covering 125 kilometres.
- Kabaddi is the national game of Bangladesh. It has no definite rules.
- Bangladesh has the fourth largest Muslim population in the world after Indonesia, Pakistan and India.

Meet the Neighbour: Bangladesh

Bangladesh is one of the most densely populated countries in the world. Located in South Asia it shares borders with India and Myanmar.

Australia and Bangladesh have a strong partnership, which is strategically and economically aligned. Bangladesh's capital city, Dhaka is 9,013 kilometres away from Australia's capital city, Canberra.

In 1971, Australia opened a High Commission in Dhaka, making it the fourth country, and the first in the developed world, to recognise Bangladesh's independence.

Two-way trade between Australia and Bangladesh has increased significantly and is now worth $2.3 billion annually. In 2017, Bangladesh exported to Australia goods such as readymade garments, woven fabrics, knitwear, textile manufactures, home textile, leather goods and footwear, processed food, fish and jute goods. Australian goods imported into Bangladesh were wheat, vegetables, lentil and pulses, milk, cream and other dairy products, cotton, fertilisers, oil seeds, primary plastic products, machinery and transport equipment, scraps and some other industrial raw materials.

History

In the late 1800s a number of Bengals arrived in Australia with retired British Indian officers. However, Bangladeshis were not counted separately in the Australian census until after 1971 and the independence of Bangladesh from Pakistan. Between 1991 and 2011 there was a large increase in arrivals. Some came to Australia under the skilled migration program, others arrived under family migration or the humanitarian program.

New South Wales has the largest Bengal community with 21,643 in the 2016 census. Over 66% of these people lived in households where the family structure is one couple with children.

At a Glance

Government

Bangladesh is a parliamentary democratic republic. Bangladesh's government is divided into three parts: the Legislative, Executive and Judiciary. The President of Bangladesh is the Head of State. The Prime Minister of Bangladesh is responsible for running the federal government. The President of Bangladesh is elected for five years. Bangladesh is a multi-party state with three major parties.

The country is divided into eight administrative divisions, 64 districts and 491 sub-districts.

The eight administrative divisions are:

- Barisal
- Chittagong
- Dhaka
- Khulna
- Mymensingh
- Rajshahi
- Rangpur
- Sylhet

Economy

Bangladesh is a developing country with the eighth fastest growing economy in the world.

Major Industries:

Major industries include textiles, steel, electronics, pharmaceuticals, shipbuilding, energy, construction materials, chemicals, ceramics, food processing and leather goods.

Main Agriculture:

Bangladesh is among the world's top producers of rice, potatoes, tropical fruits, jute and farmed fish.

Main Exports:

Bangladesh is the world's second-biggest apparel exporter after China. Other exports include footwear, jute goods, home textile and frozen shrimps and fish.

Main Imports:

Bangladesh's main imports are petroleum and oil, textile and food items. Other imports include iron and steel, edible oil, chemicals, yarn and plastic and rubber articles.

Natural Resources:

Bangladesh is the seventh-largest natural gas producer in Asia.

Australian Aid

Australian aid helps promote stability in Bangladesh. In 2018-19 Australian Official Development Assistance (ODA) will be approximately $59.8 million.

Australia's ODA supports local initiatives with a particular focus on education and building economic resilience amongst the poorest and most marginalised communities.

The main objectives of Australian aid are:

- to improve access to education and learning outcomes
- to build resilience by reducing vulnerability and finding ways to support inclusion in the growing economy
- to prioritise gender equality by focussing on empowering women and girls.

In 2016-17 Australian Aid was linked to:

- providing primary and pre-primary education services to over 20 million children. Over half of these were girls and most were from very poor families
- the distribution of textbooks, and access to quality education in areas where government schools are not operating.

In 2017, Australia also provided 64 Australia Awards to Bangladeshi students for study in a range of fields including engineering, development, public health, transport and public policy.

The People

The name Bangladesh means 'land of the Bengali people' in the Bengali language. Bangladesh covers two thirds of a geopolitical, cultural and historical region called Bengal. The other third of Bengal is divided between the Indian territories of West Bengal, Tripura and Assam's Barak Valley. Bengali people migrated to the region thousands of years ago. Bangladesh became an independent country in 1971.

Today, Bangladesh is one of the most densely populated countries in the world. The vast majority of the population are Muslim, although there are also small populations of Hindus, Buddhists and Christians. It is ethnically homogenous, with 98% of the population being Bengali. There are 27 other distinct ethnic groups that are recognised by the government, although researchers claim that the number is closer to 75. Many of these groups contain only a few thousand members. Most groups live in a region called the Chittagong Hill Tracts. Each group has its own dialect, dress and culture.

Jumma is a collective term for the 12 tribes inhabiting the Chittagong Tracts. Most are Buddhist, although there is also some Hindu and Christian groups. The Chakma are the largest of these ethnic groups. They are Therevada Buddhist.

Daily Life

Family is the focus of daily life in Bangladesh. Families are large and it is common to live with two or more generations, especially in rural areas where many generations help run farms. In cities, grandparents help care for young children so their parents can work.

Families are patriarchal, meaning the head of the family is male and makes all major decisions, including what career paths the children will take and who they will marry. Most marriages are arranged. Women are expected to obey their husbands, while children are taught to respect their elders.

Family Structure

Traditionally, Bangladeshis have lived in multi-generational joint families. The family is made up of relatives that share a common ancestor, and the wives of the men in that family. Once a woman marries, she joins her husband's family. This joint family structure was adopted out of economic necessity as well as social and cultural needs. However, for many families, a nuclear family structure has replaced the joint one.

Child Marriage

Bangladesh has the world's worst record on child marriage. The legal age to marry is 18 and yet according to UNICEF, nearly two-thirds of girls are married before the age of 18. More than a quarter of girls are married before they reach 15.

The Untouchables

The constitution of Bangladesh maintains equal rights for all people irrespective of any race, caste, creed or religion. However, the reality is quite different for many people who are born into a social class known as the untouchables. Also known as dalits, the untouchables have always been considered the lowest in society. There may be as many as 6.5 million dalits living in Bangladesh, although numbers are difficult to define because they are not recorded on the country's census. In recent years, younger dalits have been demanding changes to the systems that oppress them.

City Slums

Bangladesh's untouchables live in slums. The streets are narrow and often sewage water runs into open drains. Most areas lack basic sanitation services and often have no access to electricity or clean water. These areas can be prone to flooding and are susceptible to fire. Child labour is rife in these slums. In 2014, the government counted 14,000 slum settlements.

Students celebrating their HSC results, Dhaka, Bangladesh

Language

Bengali, also known as Bangla, is the official language of Bangladesh. Around 98% of Bangladeshis are fluent in Bengali, however there are many different dialects. English is widely spoken.

Education

Children in Bangladesh attend primary school from age 6 to 11. Primary school is compulsory and free. In recent years the enrolment rate for primary school has increased to 89% of boys and 94% of girls. However, access to education remains a challenge for many children. Only half of all children living in slums attend school.

Secondary school is generally not free and most schools are privately owned. The government provides free education to girls from rural areas in a bid to keep them in school and deter under age marriage. City schools can be well equipped but schools in rural areas often don't even have a qualified teacher. One third of staff at government schools teach without a Certificate in Education.

For those students who achieve their Higher School Certificate, some attend technical colleges or university. The University of Dhaka is the largest university in the country.

Sports

Cricket is the country's most popular sport. All over Bangladesh, in every city and every village, people play cricket. There are many cricket stadiums around the country. Poorer people will watch games on television. Even those people who don't have their own television will find one nearby for important matches. The Bangladesh national cricket team goes by the nickname, 'The Tigers', after the Royal Bengal tiger. The Tigers have played Test cricket since 2000.

Some traditional sports of Bangladesh include:

- Nouka Baich: a traditional rowing sport with teams of up to 100 members. The only rule is that the boat cannot have an engine.
- Kho Kho: a game of tag played on a rectangular field. Teams have 12 players with 9 players taking the field during play.
- Boli Khela: a traditional form of wrestling.
- Lathi Khela: a form of martial arts that uses sticks to fight.

The Sari

Bangladeshi people dress modestly. Women wear a sari (shari), which is a piece of cloth that is draped over the body in various styles. They range from simple styles to ornate silk saris for important occasions. Men wear a garment that is similar to a sarong, called a lungi. It is usually worn with a western style shirt. For more formal occasions they wear a long collarless shirt called a Panjabi. Many young people, or business people wear western style clothes.

Important Sites

As of June 2018, Bangladesh has three UNESCO World Heritage sites.

Cultural

- Historic Mosque City of Bagerhat (1985)
- Ruins of the Buddhist Vihara at Paharpur (1985)

Natural

- The Sundarbans (1997)

(There are 5 more sites currently on the Tentative List.)

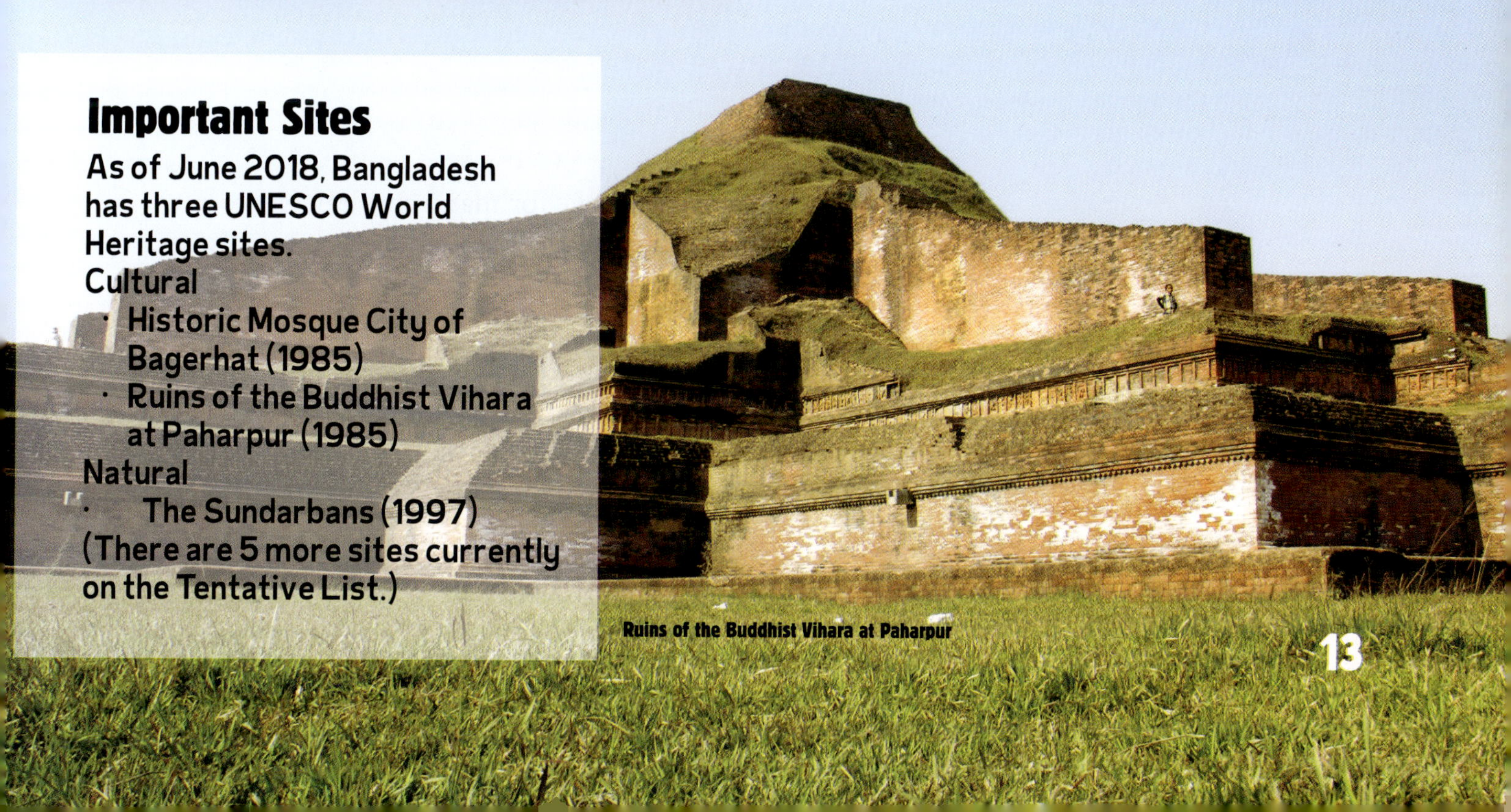

Ruins of the Buddhist Vihara at Paharpur

Health

In the past decade, Bangladesh has made great strides in improving healthcare, especially for women and children. Children are vaccinated against eight diseases: tuberculosis, diphtheria, pertussis, tetanus, polio, measles, hepatitis B and influenza. Bangladesh has been polio free since 2001. Diarrhoea now accounts for only 2% of child deaths under five, compared with almost a fifth in the 1990s. However, malnutrition, unsafe drinking water and population density still contribute to the spread of diseases such as malaria, measles, dysentery and pneumonia. Pneumonia is one of the leading causes of childhood death in Bangladesh.

Most people have access to a public hospital or, if they live in a rural area, a local health clinic in a nearby village. There is a shortage of doctors and nurses. Many of the country's recent health programs have focused largely on rural health services. The result of this is that urban healthcare is now a pressing issue. There are over 14,000 slum settlements in urban areas and the people who live there suffer from health and nutrition challenges. By 2050, more than half of the country's population is expected to reside in urban areas, therefore urban health is a major and immediate issue.

Non-communicable diseases such as diabetes, heart attack, hypertension and liver disease are on the rise with around 60% of healthcare costs borne by the patients themselves.

Women and Childbirth

Complications during childbirth are the leading causes of newborn deaths in Bangladesh. Neonatal deaths also comprise 61% of all mortality causes for children aged under five. A push to address newborn health began in 2001 and has been effective in decreasing the number of deaths. Better access to healthcare and safe caesareans, antibiotics, vaccines and trained medical professionals have been key to this.

Funding Better Healthcare

According to a report published by the World Health Organization, the healthcare system in Bangladesh relies on funding from four areas: the government, private sector, nongovernmental organisations (NGOs) and donor agencies.

Women

In 2017, The World Economic Forum ranked Bangladesh first in gender equality among South Asia nations for the second consecutive year. Bangladesh had climbed 23 places on the list since the previous year. This does not negate the many problems women face in Bangladesh today, but it does highlight the country's improvements in four key areas: education, economic participation, health and political empowerment.

Advancing educational opportunities for women has had a profound effect on the lives of Bangladeshi women. Over the last decade, marriage rates for girls under 15 dropped by more than 35% and Bangladesh plans to eradicate the practice entirely by 2021.

Over 3 million women are employed in the garment sector, and thanks to international campaigns and stringent inspections, working conditions have improved.

Bangladesh now ranks seventh in the world in the political empowerment of women. Women hold 50 seats in Bangladesh's National Parliament and 12,000 local political offices. As of 2018, the Prime Minister, Sheikh Hasina, is a woman, along with the Speaker of Parliament, the Leader of the Opposition and the Foreign Minister.

Despite these advancements, women still suffer high rates of violence and a lack of financial, educational and health opportunities. Domestic violence is considered normal by many people. Bangladesh still has one of the highest rates of child marriage in the world, with 29% of girls married before age 15 and 65% before the age of 18.

Sharia Law

For Bangladeshi Muslims, all family affairs such as marriage, divorce, alimony and property inheritance are regulated by Sharia. Islamic family law is applied through the regular court system. There are no limitations on interfaith marriages.

Religion

Bangladesh's constitution guarantees freedom of religion. The majority of the population are Muslim (89.5%) with the remainder comprised of Hindus (9.6%), Buddhists (0.5%), Christians (0.3%) and other religious groups.

The overwhelming majority of Muslims in Bangladesh are Bengali Muslims, but there are small communities of Bihari Muslims and Assamese Muslims.

Islam

Islam is practised by nearly 89.5% of all Bangladeshis and most of those subscribe to Sunni Islam. It is the world's fourth largest Muslim population after Indonesia, Pakistan and India.

There are many beautiful mosques in Bangladesh, including the Baitul Mukarram, also spelled as Baytul Mukarrom, which is the tenth largest mosque in the world. Muslims pray five times a day and their holy day each week is Friday.

Muslims believe in one god, called Allah, who gave his message to a prophet called Mohammed. The holy book is called the Koran.

Ramadan

Ramadan is the most important event on the Islamic calendar. Ramadan is a month of fasting during daylight hours to display faith to Allah. At the end of Ramadan, there is a big three-day celebration where families and friends celebrate together, called Eid-ul-Fitr, or the festival of breaking the fast.

Celebrations

Bangladeshis celebrate many important days each year. The biggest religious festival is Eid-ul-Fitr. Other Muslim Festivals include Eid-ul-Azha, Eid-e-Mialdunnabi, Muharram and shab-e-Barat. The Hindu community celebrates Durga Puja, while Christians celebrate Christmas and Buddhists celebrate Buddha Purnima.

Other days celebrated nationwide include Bengali New Year, Language Martyrs' Day (on 21 February, now also called International Mother Language Day), Independence and National Day (26 March), National Revolution and Solidarity Day (7 November), and Victory Day (16 December).

Hinduism

Hinduism developed around 4,000 years ago. There is no single founder and no specific set of teachings. While there is believed to be a single supreme being, followers worship many deities, or gods. Around 15 million people in Bangladesh identify as Hindu, making up just under 10% of the population.

Popular Hindu deities include:

- Brahma: The first of three gods in the Hindu Trinity. He is the creator of everything in the universe.
- Ganesha: This beloved deity has the head of an elephant. Hindus consider him the Remover of Obstacles and ask for his assistance on all matters in life.
- Lakshmi: This is the goddess of good fortune, wealth and well-being.
- Hanuman: He is known as the monkey king, and features in the great Hindu epic the Ramayana. Hanuman is worshipped for his unyielding devotion to Rama and is remembered for his selfless dedication.

Buddhism

In the 5th century BC, an Indian Prince called Siddhartha Guatama turned his back on his life of privilege and went on a spiritual journey. This led to the birth of Buddhism. About 0.5% of the population are Theravada Buddhists. Most live in the Chittagong division.

Christianity

Christianity arrived in the region through the Portuguese traders and missionaries, during the late 16th to early 17th centuries. The majority of the small Christian population is Roman Catholic.

Hindu celebration of a traditional festival, Dhaka

Life in Cities

Bangladesh's cities are an assault on the senses. They are noisy, polluted and densely populated. The capital, Dhaka has 10.3 million residents. Bangladesh has a growing middle-class and these families live in comfort. However many people live in poverty. More and more people are migrating to the city from rural areas to look for work, but Bangladesh's cities are ill prepared for the numbers. Basic infrastructure like water supply, electricity lines and roads cannot cope with the constant rise in numbers. More often than not these new residents find themselves struggling and living in the ever-expanding slum areas. Presently some 30% of Bangladeshis live in urban areas, but one third of them live in the slums where water, sanitation and healthcare services are quite poor.

Life in Rural Areas

Most of Bangladesh's population still lives in towns and villages, or in the countryside. Rural life can be tough, but it is community oriented. Some places are difficult to get to, so relationships with neighbours are important. Villagers live in bamboo or mud houses, clustered together. Water is collected from public boreholes or springs. Very few homes have indoor plumbing.

Over half of Bangladesh's population is employed in farming. Most are rice farmers, but wheat and jute are also common crops. Fishing is a major industry. Although agriculture is one of the country's most important industries, life is tough for farmers. Many farmers still till the land by hand. Very few of them can afford modern farm equipment. Farms are usually small plots of land, although some farmers have formed cooperatives and share labour and machinery.

Education is often seen as a luxury and children drop out of school early to help on their family farms. Other infrastructure, such as roads and healthcare are also limited.

Natural Disasters

The country's low-lying geography makes it vulnerable to flooding during the monsoon season, cyclones and other extreme weather events.

With most Bangladeshis living in rural areas and the country's economy based heavily on agriculture, weather, climate and natural disasters have a profound impact on the country's economic and social development.

The Arts

Bangladesh has rich and varied artistic traditions. Pottery is a common art form, practised by both men and women, and Bengali textiles are renowned. Music, dance and drama are important to the Bengal people.

Art

Islamic art is characterised by ornate calligraphy and designs. A number of contemporary artists have gained international recognition, including Zainul Abedin who sketched scenes from the 1943 famine.

Puppet Theatre

Puppet shows known as Putul Naach were once the most popular form of entertainment in villages, especially for children. Puppeteers depicted rural life, religious beliefs, and traditional tales and stories using string puppets. This art form hasn't been as popular in recent years but there is a push to renew its popularity before it disappears.

Music

Bangladeshi music is separated into three major traditions: classical Indian style music, folk music and contemporary music. Folk music has been especially important, with the best-known forms being Bhatiali, Baul, Marfati, Murshidi and Bhawaiya. Traditionally, folk music has been developed by village poets, and the lyrics are rich in love-lore and devotional mysticism.

Literature

Literature is very important to the Bengal people. The oldest surviving example of Bengali literature is about a thousand years old. But it was during the medieval period that Bengali literature blossomed under the patronage of Muslim rulers. Famous poets of this period include Chandi Das, Daulat Kazi and Alaol.

Toward the end of the 19th century, Bengali literature entered a modern era, introducing literary geniuses such as Rabindranath Tagore, Kankim Chandra Chattopadhyai, Kazi Ahdul Wadud, Kazi Nazrul Islam and Mir Mosharraf Hossain.

Rabindranath Tagore

The most famous Bengali writer is Rabindranath Tagore who won the Nobel Prize for Literature in 1913. He was introduced to theatre and literature by his father, a well-known Hindu philosopher and social reformer. He wrote his first poem when he was seven.

He became a painter, poet, playwright, essayist and composer. He travelled extensively, visiting more than thirty countries, sharing his love of literature. His writings greatly influenced Bengali culture during the late 19th century and early 20th century. He introduced colloquial language and new forms of prose and verse into Bengali literature.

In 1913, he won the Nobel Prize in Literature. He was selected for his translated works, and his 1912 work of poems named Gitanjali: Song Offerings. He was the first Asian ever to win this prize.

Key Moments in History

12th century

Arab merchants arrived in Bengal and Islam began to spread.

16th century

The Mughal Empire was founded in 1526 by Babur, a descendant of Genghis Khan. Babur and the successive Mughal rulers built great cities and oversaw important works of art. The Mughal Empire took control of Bengal and the city of Dhaka became an important centre of the Mughal administration.

Prior to Independence

The British ruled the Indian subcontinent from the late 18th century until 1947 when India's independence movement succeeded.

As the British quit colonial India, they partitioned the country based on religion. Over the next two decades, approximately nine million Hindus and Sikhs moved into India and five million Muslims to Pakistan. It was one of the largest forced migrations in history and left over 14 million people displaced and and hundreds of thousands of people dead.

During this time East Pakistan and West Pakistan were established either side of India. The two provinces were separated from each other by more than 1,500 kilometres of Indian territory. The divide between the two territories was more than just geographical. West Pakistan dominated East Pakistan economically. Much of the income generated in East Pakistan was used for West Pakistan's war in Kashmir. Also East Pakistan, which was at least 15% non-Muslim (mainly Hindus), was more liberal. Bengalis had a proud literary and cultural heritage in which Muslim, Hindu and Christian writers were all held in high esteem.

A separatist movement developed in East Pakistan and in 1971, civil war erupted. An estimated 10 million East Pakistani civilians fled to India, while West Pakistan attempted to crush East Pakistan's bid for independence. In December, India invaded East Pakistan in support of the East Pakistani people and West Pakistan surrendered. East Pakistan became the independent country of Bangladesh on 16 December 1971.

Nobody knows exactly how many people were killed during the Independence War, but researchers estimate between 300,000 and 500,000 people died. The Bangladesh government puts the figure at three million.

Prime Minister Khaleda Zia

Khaleda Zia was the First Lady of Bangladesh, married to President Ziaur Rahman, one of the leaders of Bangladesh's fight for independence. After his assassination in 1981, she became the first female prime minister in Bangladesh. She was one of the first two women prime ministers in Asia, after Benazir Bhutto of Pakistan.

In the free elections, she became the prime minister of Bangladesh in 1991 until 1996 and then again from 2001 to 2006. Education was one of her main interrests and she made primary education compulsory and free for everyone, and secondary education free for girls.

Timeline of Key Dates in Bangladesh's History

1947: British colonial rule over India ends. A largely Muslim state comprising East and West Pakistan is established, either side of India. The two provinces are separated from each other by more than 1,500 kilometres of Indian territory.

1971: After a nine-month war, East Pakistan gains independence from Pakistan and becomes Bangladesh.

1973: The first parliamentary elections give the Awami League a landslide victory.

1975: Bangladesh's independence leader and first president, Sheikh Mujibur Rahman, is assassinated in a military coup.

1979: Ziaur Rahman's Bangladesh Nationalist Party (BNP) come to power.

1981: Ziaur Rahman is assassinated.

1982: General Ershad assumes power in army coup. He suspends the constitution and political parties.

1991: The country returns to a parliamentary system of government. Khaleda Zia, widow of former President Ziaur Rahman, is elected prime minister.

2014-17: Bloggers, atheists and secular intellectuals suffer from a campaign of violence by Islamists.

2016-17: An estimated one million Rohingya Muslims flee military action in Myanmar's Rakhine state and seek refuge in Bangladesh.

Food and Cuisine

Bengali cuisine is similar throughout the region, with some geographical and religious influences depending on whether you are in West Bengal or Bangladesh.

The country is weaved with rivers, so fish is a staple food. Main fish dishes include butterfish, pangas catfish, clown knifefish, walking catfish, and barramundi. The national fish is paddar ilish (hilsa from the Padma River). Fish heads are popular, and serving the fish head is a gesture of hospitality.

Other staples include rice, mutton, goat, lentils and deep fried vegetables. Bangladesh is famed for having some of the hottest dishes in the world. Mustard oil is an important ingredient. Bangladeshi cuisine incorporates the use of pastes. Green or red chilli peppers, ginger, garlic, turmeric, onion, cinnamon, coriander, cumin, or mustard seed are used in pastes. Common vegetables are cauliflower, cabbage, peas, tomato, potato, beans, carrot, radish, pumpkin, and eggplant.

Traditionally, meals were served on the floor and eaten with fingers rather than cutlery. These days, many families use tables and chairs, however food is still eaten with fingers rather than forks.

Quench Your Thirst

Popular drinks in Bangladesh include tea, coconut juice, sugar cane juice, and the yoghurt drink, *lassi*.

Etiquette Alert!

Do not use your left hand to eat! Bangladeshis consider the left hand to be unclean. (It's the hand they use when they go to the toilet.) This probably makes life difficult for people who are naturally left-handed.

Muslim Diet

Halal, the Islamic dietary standard, is prevalent across Bangladesh. Halal foods are food items that Muslims are allowed to eat and drink, because they have been prepared in a special way. Muslims do not eat pork or pork products.

On the Menu

Paratha
A fried flatbread usually eaten at breakfast.

Rotti
A baked, soft flatbread, which can also be fried.

Begun Bhaja
Fried, sliced eggplant with turmeric and salt.

Sabzi
A mixed vegetable dish with spices such as ginger, garlic, onion, cumin, and chilli pepper pastes, fenugreek, fennel seed, black cumin, ajwain, and methi.

Chicken curry
A Bangladeshi style garam masala-based curry with chicken and potatoes.

Daal
A popular lentil and spice dish that is a Bangladeshi staple.

Pulao
Rice cooked with bay leaf, cinnamon sticks and topped with crispy dried onion.

Singara
Spiced potatoes and vegetables in a pastry pocket.

Samosa
Potatoes, onions, peas, coriander, and lentils in pastry triangles.

Geography and Climate

Bangladesh covers 147,960 square kilometres and much of the year the landscape is lush and green. It is characterised by two distinct land areas: a large delta where three rivers – one of them the Ganges – meet the Indian Ocean, and hilly regions in the south-eastern and north-eastern parts of the country.

Three Rivers

Three huge rivers flow through Bangladesh. They are the Ganges, the Meghna and the Jamuna. These rivers form the largest delta in Asia, which makes the land flat and fertile. Because Bangladesh is so flat, the rivers often flood, especially during monsoon season. This makes life very difficult for the Bangladeshi people. However the silt from these floods contributes to Bangladesh having some of the most fertile soils in the world.

Chittagong Hill Tracts

Bangladesh doesn't have many mountains. Some hills rise to around 600 metres in the Chittagong Hill Tracts. This area is home to indigenous people and hill tribes.

Cox's Beach

On the southeast coast near a town called Cox's Bazar, is the longest continuous stretch of beach in the world. It runs about 120 kilometres in length, parallel to the forests of the Chittagong Hill Tracts.

Climate

Bangladesh has subtropical monsoon climate. There are three distinct seasons: a hot, humid summer from March to June; a cool, rainy monsoon season from June to October; and a cool, dry winter from October to March. Bangladesh gets monsoon rain that sweeps across the country for three months of the year.

The Great Ganges

The revered Ganges River rises in the Himalayas and flows 3,877 kilometres east to the Bay of Bengal. Human development has replaced all the original natural vegetation. The Ganges supports one of the world's highest densities of humans on earth. It suffers from extreme pollution and, from the source, a glacier called Gangotri Glacier, the impact of climate change.

Fabulous Flora and Fauna

Much of Bangladesh's natural world has been destroyed during the country's rapid development, with only 9% of forest cover remaining. The three main forest regions are the Madhupur jungle, the mangrove tidal forest along the coastal Sundarban, and the tropical rain forest of the Chittagong Hills. Bamboos, rattan, fern and grasses are all home to a rich variety of creatures.

There is an abundance of bird life, with around 525 recorded species including owls, magpies, robins, cuckoos, hawks, crows, kingfishers, parrots, woodpeckers, and mynas.

There are over 200 species of mammals in Bangladesh, with the most well-known being the national animal, the Royal Bengal Tiger. There are also numerous species of leopard, buffalo, deer and monkey. There are about 200 species of marine and freshwater fish and 150 species of reptiles including various turtle species, crocodiles, and python.

Critically Endangered Species

The species listed as Critically Endangered in Bangladesh are:

- Bengal tiger
- leopard
- hog deer
- clouded leopard
- Malayan sun bear
- Asian elephant
- hoolock gibbon
- Chinese pangolin
- long-tailed macaque
- Phayre's leaf monkey
- Asiatic black bear
- Eurasian otter
- smooth-coated otter
- Indian pangolin
- gaur
- sambar
- Himalayan striped squirrel

Transport

Bangladesh is developing economically, and improvements to transport infrastructure have been made, but there is still a long way to go. The road network needs improvement and its transport systems are out-dated and crowded. Most people ride bicycles or walk, or use the country's crowded public transport system. Another popular mode of transport for shorter journeys is a human-pulled rickshaw or motorised rickshaws, called CNGs because they are run on natural gas.

Road

Bangladesh has nearly 21,500 kilometres of road, of which 18,202 kilometres is paved. While many rural areas struggle with minimal infrastructure, Bangladesh's major cities and urban areas have highways. Car ownership has risen and Bangladesh's cities are congested and chaotic.

Railways

Rail transport in Bangladesh began on 15 November 1862. Today, 2,855 kilometres of track carry around 70 million passengers and 3 million tonnes of freight each year.

Bangladesh Railway has recently purchased ten locomotives and 200 train carriages to upgrade its aging rail transport.

The Most Crowded Train in the World

Each January, the Bishwa Ijtema festival is situated by the banks of River Turag, Tongi, Bangladesh. Millions of Muslims gather here to pray. The Bishwa Ijtema Special Train services take many attendees there and back to Dhaka. The train is known as the most crowded train in the world.

Air Transport

Bangladesh is a small country, with short distances between cities, but highly congested and accident-prone highways and slow railway and waterways means domestic air travel demand is increasing. Cargo aviation is also playing a vital role in the trend towards globalisation in the 21st century. In recent years, air transport by Bangladeshi businesses has increased with readymade garments and produce air shipped to their international destinations.

Biman Bangladesh Airlines is the flag carrier of Bangladesh. Its main hub is at Shahjalal International Airport in Dhaka. The other two international airports in Bangladesh are Chittagong and Sylhet.

Water Transport

Bangladesh has a network of inland waterways running 8,000 kilometres. They are the only mode of transport for 12% of the country's rural communities. Boats carry about 194 million tonne of cargo and roughly 25% of all of Bangladesh's passenger traffic each year. However, boats are badly maintained and most river port facilities are dilapidated with unsafe conditions. Bangladesh Regional Waterway Transport Project 1 is working to improve the navigability and safety of 900 kilometres of inland waterways. In 2017, the country's merchant navy consisted of 306 ships.

Flags, Symbols and Emblems

Flag of Bangladesh

The Bangladeshi flag is green with a red circle. The red circle is offset slightly so it appears to be in the centre when the flag is flying. The colour green represents the lush landscape of Bangladesh. The red circle symbolises the sun rising over Bengal, and also the blood of those who died for the independence of Bangladesh. The Flag of Bangladesh was adopted in 1972.

The National Emblem

Bangladesh's national emblem is a water lily surrounded by two sheaves of rice. The water lily represents the many waterways in Bangladesh. Rice represents agriculture.

Above the water lily are four stars and three jute leaves. The four stars represent the four founding principles in the first constitution of Bangladesh in 1972: territory, population, sovereignty and government.

The national emblem was adopted shortly after independence in 1971.

National Anthem

Amar Shonar Bangla is the national anthem of Bangladesh.

National Flower

Water lily

National Bird

Oriental magpie robin

National Animal

Royal Bengal tiger

Find Out More

Primary and Secondary Sources

A primary source is information created by someone who was a part of or witnessed the historical event first hand. Primary sources are very important to historians researching events and time periods. Examples of primary sources are letters, emails, filmed interviews and clips, journals and diaries, census statistics, government documents, art and maps (from the time period), the news (both print and film), photographs and maps.

A secondary source is when someone who did not actually witness the event retells the facts that someone else told them. Examples of secondary sources include news (both print and film), interviews, letters, journals and diaries, biographies, textbooks and paraphrased quotations.

READ

- *Rickshaw Girl* by Mitali Perkins

Glossary

BISHWA IJTEMA:	A gathering of millions of Muslims
BUDDHISM:	A religion based on the teachings of Buddha
CASTE:	a division of society based on differences of wealth, privilege, or race
CLIMATE CHANGE:	a shift in the planet's weather and climate patterns
CULTURE:	practices, beliefs and customs of a society or people
DALIT:	an untouchable, someone from a low class
DELTA:	forms from deposits of sediment carried by a river that splits into different branches before heading to sea
ENDANGERED:	when a species is at risk
ETHNIC GROUP:	people who share a common culture, language and heritage
HIGHLANDS:	a mountainous or elevated region
MATCHMAKER:	someone who arranged a marriage on behalf of the bride and groom's family.
MONSOON:	a season of heavy rain
PLATEAU:	large, flat area found in higher regions
RICKSHAW:	small passenger vehicle pulled by someone running or riding a bike
SUSTAINABILITY:	to support the environment
TUK TUK:	motorised rickshaw

Index